National Park Service
U.S. Department of the Interior

Sequoia and Kings Canyon National Parks
California

Sequoia and Kings Canyon
Sequoia Shuttle System:
Evaluation of First-Year Operations

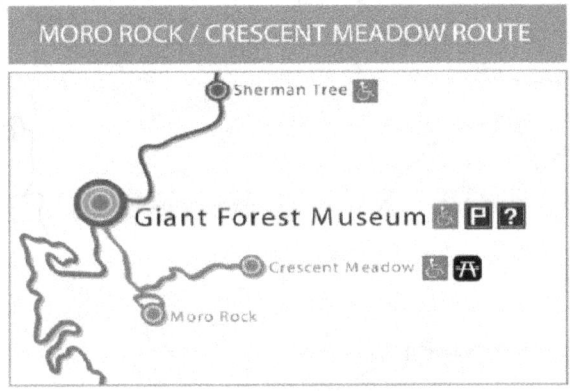

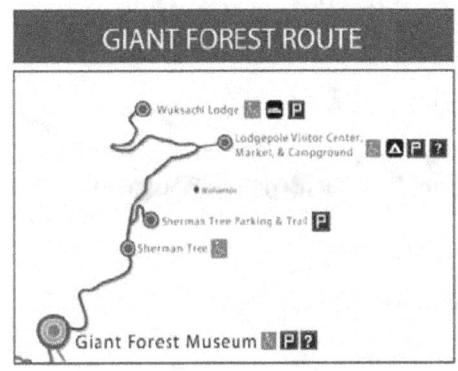

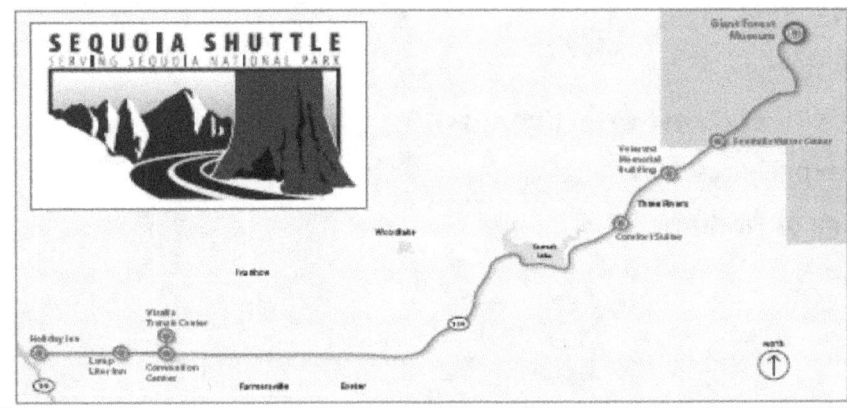

February 2008

John A. Volpe National Transportation Systems Center
Research and Innovative Technology Administration
U.S. Department of Transportation

Contents

Report notes and acknowledgments

This report was prepared for the National Park Service (NPS) Washington Service Office (WASO) by the U.S. Department of Transportation John A. Volpe National Transportation Systems Center. David Spiller, MS. Trans. Eng., of the Service and Operations Planning Division, was both project manager and principal investigator.

This effort was undertaken in support of the Alternative Transportation in Parks and Public Lands (ATPPL) Program. This effort was conducted under NPS/Volpe Center Reimbursable Agreement HW1M, as part of the Alternative Transportation Systems (ATS) Evaluations task.

The author wishes to thank the numerous organizations and individuals who graciously provided their time, knowledge, data and guidance in the development of this report. Those of particular note are listed below:

NPS/WASO
Mark Hartsoe, Park Roads Program Manager
Kevin Percival, Chief Planner, ATPPL Program

U.S. DOT/Volpe Center
Gary Ritter, NPS Program Coordinator
Melissa Laube, Senior Transportation Planner

Sequoia and Kings Canyon National Parks
Craig Axtell, Superintendent
Russ Wilson, Deputy Superintendent
Dean Butterworth, Sequoia North District Interpreter
Sequoia NPS staff who collected the data at the park at the request of the Volpe Center

City of Visalia
Monty Cox, Transit Manager
Leslie Caviglia, Deputy City Manager
Anguiano Gamaliel, Transit Analyst
Sequoia shuttle staff (drivers, dispatch, maintenance)

Executive summary

In the summer of 2007, the Giant Forest area of Sequoia National Park started up two alternative transportation services for visitors: an intra-park shuttle bus with two routes running from the Giant Forest Museum, and an external shuttle linking the park with nearby gateway communities. This report presents a multi-dimensional evaluation of the transportation service during its first season of operation.

The information and findings in this report come from a mixture of on-site data collection (e.g. for passenger counts, bus run times, parking lot usage, and vehicle counts); qualitative discussions with NPS staff, City of Visalia staff, and transportation operators; a before-and-after comparison with relevant 2002 data; and a survey of trail users at Sequoia.

Results are summarized below, grouped by topic area.

System performance and operations
Sections 4 through 7 of the report provide detailed information on bus travel times, schedule adherence, and passenger on/off patterns by route, direction of travel, and time of day. Overall, variations in the buses' travel times were generally within an acceptable range, and there were no problems with passenger loads exceeding the capacity of the buses. However, the data do indicate that Route 1 of the intra-park shuttle (Giant Forest Museum to Wuksachi Lodge) had some difficulty with schedule adherence: actual travel times along the route were sometimes too long for the buses to be able to keep to their 15-minute schedule.

Ridership
About 13 percent of visitors used the shuttle during the period in which it was operating. Total ridership for the system was 137,575 for the season, which is roughly equivalent to about 1300 one-way rides per day, or 661 visitors using the shuttle each day. Ridership was lower than some of the planning studies had forecast, but it was still substantial, and within a range that is typical for alternative transportation systems at other NPS units.

Effects on vehicle traffic and parking
Based on a comparison of traffic counts between 2002 (pre-shuttle) and 2007 (with the shuttle in operation), the bus system was associated with roughly a 20 percent drop in total traffic within the park, representing about 51,000 vehicle-miles removed from park roads. Analysis of parking lot turnover showed that visitors were leaving their vehicles parked for longer periods, on average, which is consistent with their using the intra-park shuttle rather than their own vehicles.

Environmental and resource impacts
Changes in air quality were not measured directly, but were modeled based on the reduction in motor vehicle traffic noted above. Emissions avoided were estimated at 55,000 pounds of carbon dioxide (the principal greenhouse gas), 168 kg of hydrocarbons, 1254 kg of carbon monoxide, and 83 kg of oxides of nitrogen. The reduced traffic also represented a savings of an estimated 2790 gallons of gasoline. While no direct measurements were made for changes in noise levels, the 20 percent reduction in traffic is presumed to have produced a reduction, or at worst no net change, in road noise. Use of the shuttle system also allowed a reconfiguration of the parking lots to reduce resource damage.

Safety
No safety issues arose during the period of operation, and the shuttle vehicles were not involved in any crashes.

Financial viability and cost-effectiveness

The transportation system required upfront capital expenses of about $1.1 million (primarily for buses) and $850,000 for operations. When grants received and transportation fee revenues are compared against these costs (with the capital costs annualized), the system ran a small surplus.

For the intra-park shuttle, total costs were in the range of $3-4 per one-way passenger trip. The external shuttle to gateway communities, with its much longer travel time and lower ridership, cost about $60 per one-way trip. However, the external shuttle is an important feeder to the intra-park system, ensures that visitors keep their cars out of the park altogether, and contributes the greatest reduction in vehicle mileage.

Overall, the "productivity" of the system averaged 22 boarding passengers per vehicle per hour. This is below the average (34.8) for public bus transit systems in the U.S., but is reasonable for a park (rather than urban) environment.

Impacts on visitor experience

No formal survey was conducted to assess visitors' experience or satisfaction with the shuttle system. However, one of the Park's goals for the system was to expand access to the hiking trails by allowing visitors to take a one-way hike and return to their vehicle via the shuttle (or vice versa). A limited survey of trail users showed that about 30 percent had used the shuttle, which is significantly higher than the overall rate and suggests that hikers did indeed take advantage of these new options.

Section 1: Purpose

This report presents an evaluation of the first-year start-up (system was operational mid-May to mid-September 2007) of the visitor shuttle system in the Giant Forest area of Sequoia National Park (SEKI). The visitor shuttle system design also includes an external shuttle or transit link, connecting the gateway communities of Visalia and Three Rivers to the park.

The evaluation is intended to determine the impact of the visitor shuttle system on the goals, objectives and design criteria set forth by the park in a long history of both park management planning and derivative or tiered transportation project-specific planning. These are summarized below:

- Improve traffic flow and safety by reducing congestion on Generals Highway, particularly within the Giant Forest area of the national park;

- Reduce parking space demand and congestion at key park tourism sites, including General Sherman Tree, the Giant Forest Museum, Moro Rock, and Crescent Meadow;

- Preserve environmental resources: reduce air pollution and noise;

- Enhance the visitor experience by providing options to driving and parking under congested conditions, expanding opportunities for combining bus access with walking and hiking, and improving environmental management.

- Allow for future growth in visitation compatible with preservation of park natural resources, i.e., carrying capacity

- Provide financially sustainable, cost-effective service affordable to visitors and NPS.

The evaluation is based on only data that was collected by the City of Visalia, which operated the visitor shuttle system, and by park staff. At the request and direction of the U.S. DOT Volpe Center, the park staff and the City of Visalia collected an additional set of data. The evaluation is also informed by on-site observation (at the mid-point of the operating season), and discussion with staff from the City of Visalia and the park. In broad outline, it conforms to the evaluation plan, but it is constrained by what data are available and limitations and reliability of that data. However, it does include analysis of new data that was collected to assess impacts – the identification of which could be considered a modification to the evaluation plan dictated by the on-site visit and observation of the system.

Section 2: Project history

[This section is based on McDonald Transit Associates, Inc.'s *SEKI Shuttle Implementation Study* (2005) which reviewed and summarized the project history to that point.]

Modern planning for the Sequoia visitor shuttle began in 1971 with the *Master Plan for Sequoia and Kings Canyon National Parks*. The plan established two paramount goals for the area: enhance resource protection and improve visitor experiences. A 1974 preliminary plan was proposed to the public that called for removing major development from the Giant Forest sequoia grove. It also called for establishing a public transportation system "to minimize private vehicular traffic" and to provide access to the Giant Forest "for interpretive means."

These early planning efforts and public meetings led to the production of the 1980 *Giant Forest Lodgepole Development Concept Plan (DCP)*. This was a significant document that contained several important recommendations. These include converting the Giant Forest to a day use only area within 10 years; consolidating day use parking at a large, central location; closing the Crescent Meadow Road and instituting a visitor shuttle. This plan was adopted and by 1984 line item construction funding began arriving at SEKI. Known as Package 200, approximately $70 million has been spent to date assuming the eventual implementation of a visitor shuttle. Shuttle stops have been constructed as part of this effort. In 1993, park management convinced the concessionaire to operate a visitor shuttle linking Lodgepole to Crescent Meadow. Service operated every 30 minutes with funding provided through a pass-through addition to room rates. The shuttle continued through the 1990s.

Efforts to implement the recommendations of the 1980 DCP in the Giant Forest were initiated in 1994 and culminated in the 1995 *Draft Interim Management Plan/Environmental Assessment*. The primary question addressed in this effort was how to interface Park features and facilities with parking areas and a transportation system. A consultant produced a report analyzing traffic and parking conditions and transportation demand. The resulting *Visitor Transportation System Analysis (June 1995)* produced transportation system alternatives. Common to all alternatives was a lodging shuttle connecting Wuksachi and Lodgepole to the Giant Forest. There was no preferred alternative. In April 1996, the NPS approved the final *Interim Management Plan*. The plan included the current parking configuration, improving parking at Upper Sherman Tree and a two route shuttle system. The plan effort included public comment analysis that showed strong support for the visitor shuttle system.

In 1998, detailed planning began for the implementation of the shuttle. A consultant prepared a *Transportation Condition Assessment* in 1999. It documented congestion and access problems in the Giant Forest and described a visitor shuttle system as a solution. In summer 2001, another consultant produced a detailed operating plan for the shuttle. This led to a November 2001 decision by the Transportation Advisory Group (TAG) as part of the NPS' national Alternative Transportation Program to recommend a more detailed analysis prior to implementation. This analysis was performed in 2003 by Otak, Inc. (Otak). It too collected baseline data, and found a need for the shuttle and provided detailed plans for implementation of the shuttle and a parking management system. This effort also provided analysis and recommendations regarding regional public transportation links to the parks through partnerships in the local community.

In 2004, the recommendations of the Otak report were re-evaluated by NPS staff. After a meeting at SEKI, the concept of a "core route" serving only the General Sherman Tree and Giant Forest Museum was suggested as a more affordable initial phase of service. Analysis of this concept and an evaluation of the cost and service estimates in the Otak report were the genesis of the scope of work for the McDonald Transit Associates study, the latest (and last) planning and design effort which forms the basis for the current implementation.

Actual actions undertaken by the park and the City of Visalia before the start-up operations in 2007, consonant with prior conceptual plans for a visitor shuttle system in support of overarching general management plan goals of resource protection, include:

- Construction of the Upper Sherman Tree parking lot and shuttle stop.

- Shuttle stop construction at Wuksachi, Lower Sherman Tree and Giant Forest Museum.

- Conceptual proposal from the City of Visalia to provide the shuttle service.

- Acquisition of Federal Congestion Mitigation Air Quality (CMAQ) funds by the City of Visalia to operate the service.

Section 3: New data collection by SEKI and Visalia

In response to the request and technical direction from the U.S. DOT Volpe Center (see Appendices), the park collected in accordance with established data collection protocols the additional data items below:

- Parking duration surveys were conducted every 1/2 hour from 9 a.m. until 5:30 p.m. at the Giant Forest Museum and Upper Sherman Tree parking lots from Thursday, August 9th through Sunday, August 12th.

- Traffic counts were conducted on the Crescent Meadow / Moro Rock road in 15 minute increments from 9 a.m. until 6 p.m. over the same four day period.

- Parking lot surveys were conducted at the Moro Rock and Crescent Meadow parking areas at approximately 10 a.m., 12 p.m., 2 p.m., and 4 p.m., Thursday through Sunday. At Moro Rock a tally was taken of cars parked in the lot and vicinity; at Crescent Meadow the last three digits of the license plate of each car parked in the lot was collected. The turn-over at Moro Rock was 100% between the two hour sampling period.

- Hiker intercept surveys were conducted at the Crescent Meadow trailhead on Thursday, Friday and Sunday from approximately 12 p.m. to 5 p.m. An intercept survey was unable to be conducted on Saturday due to another incident in the park that required some of the personnel that were assigned to the survey work to be assigned to that incident.

- Total numbers of vehicles travelling through the construction zone during each traffic control cycle on Generals Highway were recorded.

- Tracy Thetford, the park's Fee and Revenue Business Manager, confirmed actual occupancy rates of vehicles entering the park (with supporting backup data).

The City of Visalia conducted a one-week random sample of bus runs at mid season (i.e., Aug. 7-12) for the intra-park shuttle routes, i.e., Route 1 Giant Forest Museum to Lodgepole/Wuksachi and Route 2 Giant Forest Museum-Moro Rock-Crescent Meadow (see route schematics in Figures 1 and 2 respectively). Data collected included: boarding and alighting data by stop, time of arrival by stop, vehicle-miles and passenger-miles, passengers on-board the vehicle between inter-stop segments of the route, total travel time for the run, and number of bus runs sampled by time-of-day.

Section 4: System characteristics

Based on the on-site visit, direct observations, and discussions held with park and City of Visalia staff a synoptic summary of the essential characteristics of the visitor shuttle system and its operations are presented below. One of the appendices ("Seeing Sequoias by Shuttle") provides additional detail on the shuttle system.

1. Intra-park routes: Route 1 (Giant Forest Museum- Wuksachi Lodge/Lodgepole), - every other run goes to Wuksachi Lodge (30 minute frequency); every run serves Lodgepole (15 minute frequency)
2. Vehicle used on Route 1: El Dorado 40' 36 passenger seats; Visalia bought used vehicles (5 years old, 2002)
3. Intra-park routes: Route 2 (Giant Forest Museum – Crescent Meadow) – Vehicle used on route is a Starcraft Cutaway, using an E450 Super Duty chassis – 16 passengers, 12 with 2 wheelchairs;
4. Visalia to Sequoia Shuttle: Uses same vehicle as Route 2; 5 runs in the morning and 5 runs in the afternoon
5. Giant Forest Museum is the central transportation hub for the system, facilitating passenger transfers between all three routes.
6. Vehicles for the Visalia to Sequoia Shuttle stored at Visalia, because need to dispatch and cover the 5 runs in the morning (2 ½ hours each way travel time!)
7. Vehicles for Route 1 (4 needed to cover schedule, 1 spare) are stored at Lodgepole; 3 vehicles for use on Route 2 and for use on Visalia to Sequoia Shuttle are also stored at Lodgepole (but can be switched out with the vehicles at Visalia, since same vehicles are used for both routes).
8. Vehicles and drivers on the Visalia to Sequoia Shuttle complete their morning run to the park, then will conduct several runs on Route 2 before making return trip to Visalia on the Visalia to Sequoia Shuttle
9. Small vehicles: 3 spares; Large vehicle: 1 spare; Note: small vehicle can if necessary be briefly deployed on Route 1, but large vehicle can NOT be deployed on Route 2
10. Maximum number of vehicles in service concurrently: 5 small vehicles (2 on Visalia to Sequoia Shuttle, and 3 on Route 2), and 4 large vehicles; total fleet size is 13 vehicles (5 large, 8 small)
11. In morning, to start service 1 large vehicle is deadheaded from Lodgepole to Wuksachi Lodge and then proceeds in passenger service to Giant Forest Museum; the other large vehicle is deadheaded from Lodgepole to Giant Forest Museum and then proceeds in passenger service to Wuksachi Lodge; additional 2 vehicles are then added to service to meet 15 minute schedule on Route 1 to Lodgepole (30 minute schedule to Wuksachi Lodge)
12. Route 2: 45 minute cycle time (hence 3 vehicles need to meet 15 minute headways)
13. Vehicles deadheaded to Giant Forest Museum from Lodgepole to start Route 2 service until vehicles arrive from the Visalia to Sequoia Shuttle at Giant Forest Museum
14. Enough slack in schedule to reasonably maintain schedule on Route 2, but not enough slack in schedule on Route 1 to adequately maintain schedule.
15. Vehicles have voice communications with transit control/dispatch center at Lodgepole (some 'dead' spots)

Section 5: System performance

As mentioned, data for a one-week random sample of bus runs were collected the week of August 7, 2007. The sample bus runs[*] for Routes 1 and 2 of the intra-park shuttle have been organized into sub-samples by route, direction and time period. These are illustrated in Table 1 below. This 'data block design' has been used to organize the one performance metric for system performance for which data were collected: route travel time and its variation. These 'data block' sub-samples have also been used as a basis to compute and construct an *average passenger load profile* by route, direction and time period (see section 7).

Table 1
Data block sample design (run # in sample)

Time period	Route1 GFM-WUK	Route 1 WUK-GFM	Route 2 GFM-CM-GFM
AM	9,28	5,6,18,23	13,19,29
Midday	2,22,24	1,14,20	10,15,26,30
PM	8,11,21	12,16	3,4,7,17,25,27,31

When the sample bus runs are organized in this fashion, it does appear that some sub samples are 'over represented' while other sub samples are under represented. Nevertheless, the random sample (small as it is) and associated sub samples provide useful, indicative information characteristic of the visitor shuttle operation.

The measured travel time (TT) for each route, direction and time period and its variation (using as a metric the Range= Max TT – Min TT) are illustrated in Table 2, below.

Table 2
Travel time (TT) and variation in travel time for sampled runs
(range variation = max TT – min TT) [1]

Time period	Route1 GFM-WUK	Route 1 WUK-GFM	Route 2 GFM-CM-GFM
AM	30 27 Range Variation = 3 minutes	45 41 42 48 Range Variation = 7 minutes	35 35 31 Range Variation = 4 minutes
Midday	38 31 30 Range Variation = 8 minutes	34 36 15 Range Variation = 19 minutes	30 33 40 40 Range Variation = 10 minutes
PM	40 31 30 Range Variation = 10 minutes	31 36 Range Variation = 5 minutes	31 31 36 25 30 25 27 Range Variation = 11 minutes
Weighted Average Range Variation[2]	7.5	10.55	9.21

Notes: 1. Travel time (TT) presented is for the sampled bus runs identified in the sub-samples illustrated in Table 1.
2. Weighted by the number of runs in each sub-sample.

[*] Total number of bus runs in the sample equaled 31. In the computer printout provided by the city of Visalia, each sampled bus run was numbered by the Volpe Center and those numbers are reflected in Table 1.

No data were collected to permit a decomposition of the variation in travel time along Routes 1 and 2 attributable to fluctuations in road traffic conditions versus fluctuations in passenger boardings at the shuttle stops. The results illustrated in Table 2 do seem to corroborate the conclusions of the transit dispatch staff – expressed during the on-site visit - that schedule adherence is more a problem for Route 1, given the length and cycle time allowed for the route and the number of large buses available for assignment to the route, than for Route 2. The transit schedule allows for a 45-minute cycle time (i.e., total round-trip time) for Route 2, and with 3 small vehicles assigned to the route (including vehicles interlined from the external shuttle), a headway of 15 minutes (and adherence to that frequency) is possible with a high degree of reliability.

Section 6: Visitation

NPS/PUSO[*] indicates that the latest data available for the number of recreational visits at Sequoia NP during the same five month operating season that the visitor shuttle ran is as follows: May: 104,572; June: 115,062; July: 162,584; August: 158,372; and September: 107,311. However, the visitor shuttle operated in May and September 2007 for approximately two weeks only in each of these two months respectively. Thus, an imputed total for the number of visitors (based on 2006 data; 2007 data is unavailable) is 541,959 – counting only one-half of the number recorded for May and September.

The number of visits in August is particularly important, because the data on traffic flow on Generals Highway was collected in August 2002 ('before' the shuttle system) and in August 2007 (('after' the shuttle system was operating) (see section 8, Traffic). NPS/PUSO show the following time trend for the August data (visitors, not vehicles): **August 2002: 169,075**; August 2003: 167,864; August 2004: 169,686; August 2005: 176,490; **August 2006: 158,372** (used as a surrogate for August 2007).

Section 7: Visitor use of shuttle system

Aggregate statistics on the use of both the external shuttle (Visalia-Three Rivers-Park) and the intra-park shuttle (i.e., Routes 1 and 2) are presented in Table 3. The metrics presented by month of operation include: total number of passengers for the external shuttle (total number of trips for the intra-park shuttle system); average number of passengers (or trips) per day; and load factor per bus run.

For the external shuttle, passengers who board the shuttle buses leave their cars in the gateway communities. The external shuttle connects with the intra-park shuttle system at Giant Forest Museum, where passenger transfers between park routes and between the external and intra-park shuttle take place. Thus, all passengers on the external shuttle take the shuttle buses into the park and out of the park, for a single round trip (or two one-way transit trips). Total number of passengers is therefore the better metric for the external shuttle. Also, because of the design of the system, all passengers on the external shuttle system transfer to the intra-park shuttle system. Therefore, data that measures the total number of trips or boardings on the intra-park shuttle system already count those passengers who transfer from the external shuttle. The trips made on the external shuttle should NOT be combined with the total number of trips made on the intra-park shuttle system (this would double count these trips).

The metric *total number of trips* (i.e., one-way transit trips which is equivalent to the total number of boardings) is the better measure for usage of the intra-park shuttle system. An **upper bound** on the number of visitors who use the intra-park shuttle system (and computation of the percent of total visitation this represents, i.e., the modal split) is to also assume that each visitor (or the vast

---

[*] See http://www2.nature.nps.gov/NPstats/dspPark.cfm

majority) takes a round-trip (i.e., two one-way transit trips) on the system. This clearly overstates the actual unique number of visitors who use the system. For example, a visitor who parks at Giant Forest Museum may then board Route 2 to Moro Rock, climb the rock, then board Route 2 again to Crescent Meadow and access the Crescent Meadow trailhead, explore on foot for awhile, then board a bus at Crescent Meadow and return to Giant Forest Museum. That same visitor may then board a bus on Route 1 to the Sherman Tree, explore that site, then take a second bus up to Wuksachi Lodge for lunch, then return to her car at Giant Forest Museum. This visitor, with the itinerary just articulated, has taken three (3) trips on Route 2 and three (3) trips on Route 1 – a total count of six (6) trips. It is not possible with the data that were collected to estimate the statistical distribution of multi-hop trips, and to adjust the number of passengers accordingly. Our best estimate is to simply assume that each visitor (or the vast majority) who used the intra-park shuttle system rode two one-way or one round trip on the system, and to not double count the passengers who transferred from the external shuttle.

Based on the above discussion, the aggregate number of trips on the shuttle system is 137,575. This represents an upper bound of 68,788 passengers or visitors. As a percent of total visitation, this represents 0.127 (68,788/541,959) or 12.7%.

Table 3
Aggregate statistics: usage of shuttle system

	External shuttle			Intra-park shuttle					
				Route 1			Route 2		
	Total # of passengers[1]	Average # of passengers per day	Load factor per run	Total # of trips	# trips per day	Load factor per run[2]	Total # of trips	# of trips per day	Load factor per run[2]
May	182	20.2	4.0	4015	446.1	12.1	2169	241	7.1
June	618	20.6	4.1	16295	543.2	14.7	8968	298.9	8.8
July	818	26.4	5.3	35076	1131.5	30.6	18005	580.8	17.1
August	876	28.3	5.7	30357	979.3	26.5	15010	484.2	14.2
September	158	39.5	7.9	5047	1682.3	45.5	2633	877.7	25.8
Totals	**2652**	**25.2**	**5.1**	**90790**	**873**	**23.6**	**46785**	**449.9**	**13.2**

Notes: 1. Source: Visalia data Excel spreadsheet, computed as the number of one-way trips/2.
2. # of runs for Route 1: 37; # of runs for Route 2: 34 (source: schedules)
3. One-way trips is a better measure of ridership for the intra-park shuttle routes because many passengers may use the shuttle on only one direction, e.g., from a trail back to their car, or use the shuttle for multiple 'hops' between visitor attractions.

Comparison of actual usage to planning estimates
It is constructive, now that actual usage data is available for the first-year operation of the shuttle system, to compare this number to planning estimates. From 2003-2006, the U.S. DOT Volpe Center provided detailed technical review of the Otak and Macdonald Transit Associates planning studies that formed the basis for the design of the visitor shuttle system. As part of that review, we also looked at alternative methods – more realistic in our view - for estimation of demand. That discussion is articulated here, augmented in the summary table by a comparison to the actual usage of the system.

The Macdonald Transit (McT) study reviews demand estimates from prior planning studies, and presents several alternative approaches to estimate ridership. McT believes the Otak numbers are overly optimistic, and ultimately McT arrives at estimates slightly lower than the Otak study (Otak: 5224 (weekend), 4567 (weekday) versus McT: 3629 (daily)). However, McT uses the same assumed modal split percentage as the Otak study to arrive at its 'conservative' estimate! Citing, however, the experience of both Rocky Mountain and Bryce in generating 0.3-0.4 transit trips per visitor, daily ridership would equal [0.3 x 468,592 visitors during 99 days of peak season operation]/99 = 1420 trips per day, and [0.4 x 468,592]/99 = 1893 trips per day. Visitor usage would be half these estimates since each visitor would be making a round trip (2 trips per visitor).

The Zion National Park Shuttle also provides an informative basis for estimating demand at SEKI. Visitors are presented with a choice option in using the Zion Town Loop or driving their personal car to the Visitor Center. At the Visitor Center, there is a mandatory transfer to the Zion Canyon Loop. Thus the numbers illustrated in the table on p. 16 of the McT study apply to the same panel of visitors in a naturalistic experiment. The numbers show that when provided a choice between use of a private vehicle and a shuttle service to the same transfer point, 65835 will use the shuttle. 401,947 use the mandatory system. Although it is not known what percent of the 401,947 visitors arrive via the gateway community (thus presented with a choice of using the shuttle or driving a personal vehicle), a lower bound for modal split for the voluntary link is ~16% (65835/401947). Assuming ~80% arrive via the gateway community of Springdale, modal split for the voluntary link would be ~ 20% (65835/321557). Daily ridership at SEKI based on a lower-bound estimate of Zion's actual modal split (not assuming a modal split) is thus [0.16 x 468,592]/99 = 757 trips per day. Since each visitor would make two (2) trips, this represents 378 visitors likely to use the SEKI shuttle.

The 2002 visitor survey cited by the McT study on p. 20 has a useful statistic to bound the number of likely users at SEKI, given the way most visitors experience the resources in the park. The survey indicated that eighty five percent (85%) of visitors come for the scenic drive, and may be unlikely to transfer to a shuttle system with less convenience and spontaneity. If the remaining 15 percent of visitors experience SEKI in a more intensive way (e.g., use of trails, and longer duration stays within the Giant Forest), then applying the 16-20% estimate of a likely modal split to this subset of visitors who might be persuaded to switch to a shuttle system yields 114 – 142 trips per day, representing 57-71 visitors using the system [(0.16 x (0.15 x 468592))/99; (0.20 x (0.15 x 468592))/99].

Table 4
Summary of Demand Estimates and Comparison to Actual Shuttle Usage

Alternative Demand Estimation Approach	Estimate of Number of Daily Transit Trips	Estimate of Number of Daily Visitors Using Shuttle System
Trip generation	1420-1893	710-947
Zion Benchmark	757-946	378-473
2002 Survey	114-142	57-71
McT Study and Approach	**3629**	**1814**
Actual Usage of System	**1322**[1]	**661**[2]

Notes: 1. Total # of trips/# of operating days in season (137,575 trips/104 days)
2. Number of daily transit trips/2

It is interesting to note that while first year usage is substantially less than the planning estimate by McT (~36 percent), shuttle usage is still substantial and best approximates the 'trip generation' rate methods based on the experience at Rocky Mountain and Bryce Canyon.

Passenger load profiles for the intra-park shuttle system
The one-week sample of bus runs collected 'on' and 'off' counts of passengers by stop. This permits construction of the passenger load profile – illustrating the on-board count of passengers on the bus along all portions of the route. The random sample of bus runs have been organized into sub-samples – see Table 1 for the list of runs in the data block sample design – by route, direction and time period. An *average passenger load profile* has been constructed in accordance with the data block sample design of Table 1. Both boarding and alighting number of passengers have been averaged by stop over the sub-sample of runs, and the passenger load profile computed accordingly

(see Attachment II for detailed methods). Thus, the *average passenger load profile* represents an average condition for a given combination of route, direction and time period, but is not equivalent to any single bus run.

Figures 1-9, with certain metrics graphically derived from the profile, are presented in detail as Attachment III.

Section 8: Traffic

Measurements were taken at the construction zone on Generals Highway and at the entrance to Crescent Meadow/Moro Rock road as a basis for comparing traffic flow on the two main (and critical roads) within the Giant Forest area of Sequoia NP 'before' and 'after' shuttle system implementation. The construction zone along Generals Highway is an appropriate screen line since there are no 'sources' and 'sinks' for traffic along the segment between the park boundary and entrance station and Giant Forest Museum. The results of the comparison for Generals Highway are presented in Table 5. As a statistical control, the corresponding data for visitation during the same months when the traffic flow data were collected (i.e., August 2002 and August 2007/2006 – latest data available)) is also presented as well as its percent change over the span of time between the two measurements. The results clearly show that the reduction in traffic flow after the visitor shuttle is in operation is significant, and is substantially greater than the secular trend of a moderate decline in level of visitation. This provides corroborating evidence that the visitor shuttle system has diverted a significant portion of visitors who otherwise would have driven their private vehicles to and through the park.

Table 5
Generals Highway Traffic Flow (vehicles per day, both directions)
Entrance Station to Giant Forest Museum

	'Before' Shuttle	'After' Shuttle	% Δ
August 2002 4-day average (Thursday thru Sunday)	963[1]	-	-
August 2002 recreational visits	169,075[3]	-	-
August 2007 4-day average (Thursday thru Sunday)	-	701 (796)[2]	-27.2 (-17.3)
August 2006 recreational visits	-	158,372[4]	-6.3

Notes: 1. Source: Otak, Inc., Part 1 of Transportation Study and Shuttle Implementation Plan, Appendix A, p. 11; computed as the sum of thru movements and turning movements onto Crescent Meadow Road.
2. Collected by SEKI staff, August 2007 at the construction zone segment under flagging traffic control operations; large number based on disparate time periods over the four days; smaller number adjusts each count to reflect counts between 7:00 AM and 3:00 PM for all four days.
3. Public Use Statistics at http://www2.nature.nps.gov/NPStats/dspPark.cfm
4. Latest data available (2007 data unavailable), at http://www2.nature.nps.gov/NPStats/dspPark.cfm

Equivalent analysis of the traffic flow data for Crescent Meadow/Moro Rock road is presented below in Table 6. This too shows a significant and substantial reduction in the flow of traffic on Crescent Meadow/Moro Rock road with the visitor shuttle system (i.e., Route 2 to Moro Rock and Crescent Meadow) in operation. The reduced flow of traffic also has beneficial consequences – beyond resource impact reduction - in reducing the parking demand at the limited parking facilities at Moro Rock and Crescent Meadow.

Table 6
Crescent Meadow-Moro Rock Road Traffic Flow
(vehicles per day, both directions)

	'Before' Shuttle	'After' Shuttle (Inbound/Outbound) Total	%Δ
8/9/07	-	(345/311) 656	-
8/10/07	-	(366/343) 709	-
8/11/07	-	(614/546) 1160	-
8/12/07	-	(491/463) 954	-
4-day Average	1108[1]	870[2]	-21.5

Notes: 1. Source: Otak, Inc., Part 1 of Transportation Study and Shuttle Implementation Plan, Appendix A, p. 11; computed as the sum of turning movements at junction of Generals Highway and Crescent Meadow-Moro Rock road.
2. Computed from data collected by SEKI staff, August 2007.

One of the key performance metrics for the shuttle system is the number of private vehicle miles travelled (VMT) removed from park roads. Traffic is a major component of the noise and visual intrusion experienced by visitors as well as a contributor of exhaust emissions affecting air quality within the park (see section 8). Approximate estimates for both the external shuttle and the intra-park shuttle have been computed based on ridership and trip length data and are presented in Table 7.

Table 7
Vehicle-miles traveled (VMT) removed from park roads

External Shuttle	Intra-Park shuttle
50,900[1]	9100[2]

Notes: 1. Passenger-miles travelled (PMT) = $\sum r_i \times dist$
    Where r_i = ridership per run
    Dist = round-trip distance between park boundary (Entrance Station) and Giant Forest Museum
    PMT/AVO = VMT
    Where AVO = average vehicle occupancy = 3 for SEKI
2. Computed from On/Off passenger counts for week of 8/6/07. Assumes calculated passenger-miles from the random sample of bus runs applies to the 10 peak season weeks, and 0.50 x peak-week passenger-miles applies for the three shoulder weeks in May and September.
    Passenger-miles (PMT) / AVO = VMT removed from park roads for the intra-park shuttle.

Because passengers who utilize the external shuttle keep their cars out of the park entirely and the distances are relatively long from the gateway communities to Giant Forest Museum - the point of departure for starting a tour throughout the park, the largest component of VMT removed from park roads is attributable to the External shuttle operation. This highlights how critical the external shuttle is to the design of the transit system.

Section 9: Environment

No road-traffic related noise measurements were taken prior to or post shuttle system implementation. That said, it is clear from the reduction in traffic flow on park roads that road-traffic related noise, on average, is qualitatively no more than and probably substantially less with the shuttle system in operation.

The issue of vehicular exhaust emissions and the effect they have on the quality of the air shed within the park is more complex. Air quality within Sequoia NP is highly influenced by emission sources outside the park's boundary, by the unique mountainous and steep valley topography, and by larger climactic forces (e.g., wind, precipitation and temperature variants).

A rough estimate, however, can be made of simply the reduction in vehicular exhaust emissions (which correlate with but are not necessarily a one-to-one correspondence with reduction in pollutant concentrations). In April 2000, EPA published emission factors for the entire in-use fleet of passenger cars. These factors are more representative of the actual performance of the fleet of cars used by visitors to Sequoia NP than controlled measurements based on a driving duty cycle from dynamometer tests. Table 8 presents these factors.

Table 8
Emission factors and fuel consumption for actual in-use passenger car fleet

Component	Emission Rate and Fuel Consumption (per mile)
Hydrocarbons	2.80 grams (g)
Carbon Monoxide	20.9 grams
Oxides of Nitrogen	1.39 grams
Carbon Dioxide[2]	0.916 pound (lb)
Gasoline	0.0465 gallon

Notes: 1. Source: US Environmental Protection Agency, Office of Transportation and Air Quality, Emission Facts, EPA420-F-00-013, April 2000.
2. Carbon Dioxide is not a regulated emission but is the transportation sector's primary contribution to climate change.

Based on these emission factors and the combined VMT reduction for the external and intra-park shuttle system, the reduction in component emissions and fuel consumption are the following: (1) hydrocarbons: 168 kilograms; (2) carbon monoxide: 1,254 kilograms; (3) oxides of nitrogen: 83.4 kilograms; (4) carbon dioxide: 54,960 pounds; (5) gasoline consumption: 2790 gallons.

Section 10: Parking

One of the key rationales and ultimately design criterion for the visitor shuttle system at Sequoia NP was that the shuttle system would permit more optimal management of limited parking facilities in a way which would be least damaging to the Giant Forest grove of sequoia trees. Thus, the lower Sherman tree parking spaces were greatly reduced, with remaining spaces dedicated to handicapped parking only; a new upper Sherman tree lot was built in a site location outside of the giant grove of trees, but with a pedestrian access path to the General Sherman Tree – a prime visitor attraction. Improvements were made to the Giant Forest Museum lower and upper levels, with the expectation that fewer visitors would park at or adjacent to Moro Rock and Crescent Meadow once the shuttle system was in place to provide access to these sites and trailheads. In the design of the shuttle system, both Upper Sherman Tree parking lot and the Giant Forest Museum parking lot would be the two major staging areas where visitors could leave their cars and transfer to the shuttle system to explore the key visitor attraction sites and to access trailheads throughout the park.

SEKI staff collected new data using a standard license plate matching protocol at both Giant Forest Museum and Upper Sherman Tree parking lots. The data were analyzed to compute two key metrics: parking turnover and average parking occupancy. Parking turnover is a measure of how frequently or intensively a parking space is utilized. Average parking occupancy is a measure of the average time or duration a car parked. The results are presented in Tables 9 and 10.

Table 9
Giant Forest Museum parking

	Parking Turnover	Average Parking Occupancy (minutes)
8/9/07	2.07[1]	75.5
8/10/07	2.48[2]	86.4
8/11/07	3.36[3]	96.6
8/12/07	3.03[4]	91.8

Notes: Source: computed from data collected by SEKI staff
  1. (385/186)
  2. (462/186)
  3. (625/186)
  4. (563/186)

Table 10
Upper Sherman Tree parking

	Parking Turnover	Average Parking Occupancy (minutes)
8/9/07	2.69[1]	88.2
8/10/07	2.50[2]	90.6
8/11/07	3.83[3]	90.6
8/12/07	3.06[4]	83.5

Notes: Source: computed from data collected by SEKI staff
  1. (654/243)
  2. (608/243)
  3. (926/243)
  4. (744/243)

As mentioned, the design of the visitor shuttle system is premised on using Giant Forest Museum and the Upper Sherman Tree parking facilities as staging areas for visitors to park their cars and transfer to the buses. Thus a working testable hypothesis is that the parking turnover should decrease and the average parking occupancy duration should increase after the shuttle system is in operation in comparison to the value of both metrics in the baseline or 'before' shuttle implementation time period. Because the Upper Sherman Tree parking lot was not yet built when the baseline (2002) data were collected, this hypothesis was testable only for the Giant Forest Museum parking lot. The results are presented in Table 11. The results confirm the working hypothesis and shuttle system design criterion by indicating that the shuttle system has altered visitor behavior – visitors are leaving their car at the Giant Forest Museum parking lot and transferring in sufficient numbers to the buses to explore the park to affect the value of these two key performance metrics. Visitor behavior and the way visitors experience the park have been altered by the shuttle system.

Table 11
Giant Forest Museum parking lot

	Before shuttle		After shuttle	
	Parking Turnover	Average Parking Occupancy (minutes)	Parking Turnover	Average Parking Occupancy (minutes)
8/10/07	3.5[1]	52.2[1]	2.48[2]	86.4[2]
8/11/07	4.23[1]	81[1]	3.36[2]	96.6[2]

Notes: 1. Source: Appendix A, Summary of New Data Collection, p. 5, Part 1 of Transportation Study and Shuttle Implementation Plan
2. Computed from data collected by SEKI staff

Section 11: Safety

Fortunately, to our knowledge, the shuttle system was not involved in any accidents.

Section 12: Finance[*]

This section presents aggregate costs and revenues for the shuttle system. Net surplus or deficit is calculated once capital costs have been annualized. For simplicity, a single 'average' capital recovery factor (CRF) is used, skewed to the asset life of the buses since the buses comprise by far the greater component of capital expenses.

Park Revenue and Grants - The Park collected a total of $889,355 in transportation fee revenue in FY2007. The transportation fee of $10 is collected from everyone paying the $20 entrance fee to enter the park. The transportation fee is not collected all year (i.e., only in the months of). It is also not collected from people who enter the park using other passes (i.e. $30 annual Sequoia and Kings Canyon National Parks Pass, the $80 Interagency Annual Pass, Interagency Senior Pass/Golden Age (available for US Citizens/permanent residents over 62) and the Interagency Access/Golden Access (available for US Citizens/permanent residents with permanent disabilities).

The park received from the Federal Transit Administration's Alternative Transportation in Parks and Public Lands (ATPPL) a grant in the amount of $125,000 to help cover the cost of leasing shuttle buses for the operation of the shuttle in FY07. The park paid for $55,100 in fuel costs to operate the shuttle. The task agreement with the City of Visalia was for $509,180. That total includes the 125,000 grant so $384,180 is the actual cost that the park incurred. Additional park expenses include $13,709 in administrative costs and $42,202 in maintenance supplies and other start-up costs. The park is currently negotiating with the City of Visalia on a modification that if approved would increase the costs by an additional $51,135.

Total Park revenue and grants - $1,014,355

Operational costs – Park share of operational costs include $55,100 in fuel costs; $13,709 in administrative costs; and $42,202 in maintenance supplies and other start-up costs. Total park share of operational costs are $111,011.

Intra-park shuttle operational costs were budgeted at $344,239 (i.e., 6375 hours x $54) but with overtime and unanticipated expenses equaled $435,315.

---

[*] Data provided by the park, and the City of Visalia.

External shuttle operational costs were $301,597.
Thus, total operational costs for the shuttle system sum to $847,923.

Capital costs – The capital costs for the intra-park shuttle are $921,961. The capital costs for the external shuttle are $184,951. Assuming a capital recovery factor of 0.12, the total annualized capital cost for the shuttle system equals $132,830.

Total annualized shuttle cost (operating and capital) equals $980,752.
Net surplus equals ($1,014,355 - $980,752) = $33,603.

Section 13: Productivity and cost-effectiveness

The best performance metric for productivity of the shuttle system is the boarding rate per vehicle-hour. The total number of trips on the system as noted in Table 1 is 137,575 (this number includes passenger trips for passengers who transferred to the intra-park shuttle from the external Sequoia-to-Park shuttle link). The total number of vehicle-hours for the intra-park shuttle system totals 6375 hours[*]. This yields an aggregate boarding rate equivalent to (137,575/6375) = 21.58 passengers per vehicle-hour. Additional productivity metrics (e.g., passengers or trips per day; load factor per bus run) are presented in Table 1.

Cost-effectiveness metrics are presented in Tables 12 and 13 for the intra-park shuttle and external shuttle respectively.

Table 12
Intra-Park Shuttle – Cost/Effectiveness Metrics
( ) = Total Cost including Annualized Capital Costs

Service Hours[1] – 6375
Operating cost per service-hour[2] - $69.52 ($86.87)
Operating cost per trip[3] - $3.22 ($4.02)
Operating cost per passenger-mile[4] - $12.15 ($15.48)
Operating cost per VMT removed from park roads[5] - $48.70 ($60.86)

Notes:
1. Source: Visalia Internal-External Expenses.xls spreadsheet
2. Computed as the ratio of internal operating expenses (including insurance and overtime) to service hours, i.e., $443,181.93/ 6375.
3. Computed as the ratio of internal operating expenses to the total number of trips on the intra-park shuttle system (from Table 3), i.e., $443,181.93/137575.
4. Computed from the one-week sample data by constructing the number of service hours and costs for the week (# of service hours x operating cost per service-hour ($69.52)) and dividing by the number of passenger-miles computed for the sample week.
5. Computed as the ratio of operating costs to VMT removed from park roads (see Table 7).

[*] Source: data provided by City of Visalia, in internal-external expense spreadsheet.

Table 13
External Shuttle – Cost/Effectiveness Metrics
( ) = Total Cost including Annualized Capital Costs

Service Hours[1] – 2933.47
Operating cost per service-hour[2] - $102.81 ($110.38)
Operating cost per trip[3] - $56.86 ($61.05)
Operating cost per VMT removed from park roads[4] - $5.92 ($6.36)

Notes:
1. Source: Visalia Internal-External Expense.xls spreadsheet.; data provided only for May, June, July – imputed August data by assuming it equivalent to July, and imputed September data for # of service hours by assuming it was equivalent to May.
2. Computed as the ratio of operating cost to service hours, i.e., $301,596.80/2933.47.
3. Computed as the ratio of operating cost to the total number of passengers x 2 (for 2 trips per passenger or 1 round-trip, from Table 3), i.e., $301,596.80/5302.
4. Computed as the ratio of operating cost to VMT removed from park roads (from Table 7), i.e., $301,596.80/50,900.

Because the number of trips on the intra-park shuttle is large, the operating cost per trip is low; conversely the operating cost per VMT removed from park roads is large. This is reversed for the external shuttle, where the operating cost per trip is large but the operating cost per VMT removed from park roads is low. Because of the more intensive use of the buses on the intra-park shuttle system, the operating cost per service-hour is lower on the intra-park shuttle system than on the external Sequoia to Park shuttle link.

Section 14: Visitor experience

No formal visitor use and satisfaction survey was administered. But one of the key design criteria for the shuttle system was its potential to enhance visitor experience by facilitating access to trailheads thereby allowing an expanded population of visitors to hike one-way along a trail and return to their cars via the shuttle. So important was this goal that the Chief of Interpretation formalized this concept in an interpretative plan widely distributed to all interpretative staff at the park. The following points were made:

To encourage visitors to experience more of the Giant Forest interpreters can suggest the following hikes to visitors. Interpreters should encourage visitors who plan on hiking in Giant

Forest to carry a trail map, and deliver other appropriate safety messages. This list is not exhaustive:

- Park at the Sherman Parking and Trail and take the trail to the Sherman Tree. Ride the shuttle from the Sherman Tree shuttle stop back to the Sherman Tree Parking and Trail shuttle stop. (Approximate distance ½ mile, time 30 - 45 minutes)
- Park at Giant Forest Museum. Ride the shuttle from the Giant Forest Museum to the Sherman Tree shuttle stop. Take the Congress Trail to the Alta Trail to the Giant Forest Museum. (Approximate distance 3 miles one-way, time 90 – 120 minutes)
- Park at the Sherman Tree Parking and Trail and take the bus to the Giant Forest Museum. At the museum transfer to the Moro Rock/Crescent Meadow route and take the trail to the Crescent Meadow Shuttle Stop. Take the Crescent Meadow Trail to the Trail of the Sequoias. Then take the Congress Trail to the General Sherman Tree and finish by taking the General Sherman Tree Trail back to their cars. (Approximate distance 3.5 – 5 miles depending on trail choices, time 3 – 4 hours)

Existing interpretive programming in the Sequoia North Interpretive District is easily integrated with the shuttle system. Visitors can use the shuttle to attend programs that are offered daily at the Lodgepole Visitor Center, the General Sherman Tree, Giant Forest Museum, Beetle Rock Family Nature Center, and Moro Rock. The Sherman Tree Talk and the Moro Vista talks seem particularly well suited for inclusion of messages regarding the shuttles potential benefits to the health of park resources. During the core interpretive programming period interpreters are assigned roving duties at the General Sherman Tree, the Giant Forest Museum and Moro Rock. During these assigned roving periods interpreters will emphasize to visitors the benefits of using the shuttle to experience the park. The Ford Transportation Interpreters will also be assigned roving duties on board the shuttle buses and at various shuttle stops to help visitors navigate the shuttle system.

Dean Butterworth

Dean Butterworth

Data were collected by park staff for a trail user intercept survey at the Crescent Meadow trailhead to provide some insight (limited) in how the shuttle has extended the access and reach of visitors who use the trails. The results are reported below in Table 14.

Table 14
Trail user intercept survey
( ) = persons

	Modal Access		Parking Lot Used (# of groups)							Boarding Shuttle Stop (# of groups)								Alighting Shuttle Stop (# of groups)							
	% POV	%Shuttle	MR	LPVC	LPCG	WUK	GFM	UST	CM	GFM	LST	UST	LPCG	LPVC	WUK	MR	CM	GFM	LST	UST	LPCG	LPVC	WUK	MR	CM
Weekday[1]	0.68 (0.63)	0.32 (0.37)	0	5	9	2	25	5	102	6	3	7	2	2	3		26	2	1	3	1	1	0	3	40
Weekend[2]	0.75 (0.73)	0.25 (0.27)	2	4	-	-	14	5	87	14	-	5	-	-	1		1	12	-	4	5	-	-	1	2

Notes:

1. Includes data collected on Thursday and Friday, 8/9/07 and 8/10/07.
2. Due to staff re-allocation because of an emergency, 'weekend' is Sunday only.

The results clearly indicate that one-third of the groups and greater than one-third of visitors who used the trailhead also used the shuttle system. Those who used the shuttle parked outside of the Crescent Meadow trailhead, while those who accessed the trailhead at Crescent Meadow generally parked there.

Section 15: Summary of findings

This section highlights key findings of the evaluation.

- Measurement of travel time variation indicates that schedule adherence is more problematic on Route 1 to Lodgepole and Wuksachi than for Route 2 (Giant Forest Museum –Moro Rock-Crescent Meadow)
- A total of 137,575 trips were made on the shuttle system; the average load factor per bus run equaled 23.6 for Route 1, and 13.2 for Route 2. The average number of persons using the external Sequoia-to-Park shuttle averaged 25.2 per day, with a corresponding load factor per run of 5.1
- An estimate of the number of daily visitors using the shuttle is 661. This compares to forecasted planning estimates of 1814.
- The average passenger load profile varied by route, direction and time period. In general, the maximum load point for Route 1 is Lower Sherman Tree (LST) shuttle stop, and for Route 2, it is Moro Rock (MOR) shuttle stop.
- Traffic flow on Generals Highway (vehicles per day both directions) dropped between 17.3 and 27.2 percent (depending on how the data is computed) after shuttle implementation.
- Traffic flow on Crescent Meadow-Moro Rock road (vehicles per day, both directions) dropped 21.5 percent after shuttle system implementation.
- Vehicle-Miles-Traveled (VMT) removed from park roads equaled 50,900 for the external shuttle link, and 9100 for the intra-park shuttle system.
- The reduction in component emissions and fuel consumption are the following: (1) hydrocarbons: 168 kilograms; (2) carbon monoxide: 1,254 kilograms; (3) oxides of nitrogen: 83.4 kilograms; (4) carbon dioxide: 54,960 pounds; (5) gasoline consumption: 2790 gallons.
- Parking turnover decreased (3.5 to 2.48; 4.23 to 3.36) and average parking occupancy duration increased (52.2 to 86.4 minutes; 81 to 96.6 minutes) after the shuttle was in operation. The results confirm the working hypothesis and shuttle system design criterion by indicating that the shuttle system has altered visitor behavior – visitors are leaving their car at the Giant Forest Museum parking lot and transferring in sufficient numbers to the buses to explore the park to affect the value of these two key performance metrics. Visitor behavior and the way visitors experience the park have been altered by the shuttle system.
- No safety issues arose during shuttle operation.
- The shuttle system is financially sustainable in that revenues and grants exceeded total operating costs (including annualized capital costs), yielding a net surplus of $33,601.
- Productivity measured by the boarding rate per vehicle-hour equaled 21.58 passengers.
- Cost effectiveness metrics show that the intra-park shuttle (Routes 1 and 2) had an operating cost per service-hour equal to $69.52 and an operating cost per trip equal to $3.22. The corresponding values for the external Sequoia-to-Park shuttle link were $102.81 and $56.86 respectively. However, the operating cost per VMT removed from park roads showed that the intra-park shuttle system had a higher vale at $48.70, while the external shuttle link had a value of $5.92.
- The trail user intercept survey indicated that more than one-third of users used the shuttle system to access the trails originating or terminating at Crescent Meadow. This is consistent with one of the design criterion for the shuttle system to expand the experience of visitors by allowing visitors to experience the trail system by allowing one-way hikes combined with shuttle access to/from their parked vehicles. It is also consistent with the park's management goals to optimize parking management and reduce resource impacts by reducing the parking demand at parking lots in sensitive areas, and shifting that demand to parking facilities more suitable to handle it.

Attachment I

Seeing Sequoias by Shuttle

From late May through early September, shuttle buses make it easier to see the Giant Forest sequoia grove every day. From the transfer stop at the Giant Forest Museum, the free Giant Forest Route (green) runs north as far as Wuksachi Lodge. The Moro Rock / Crescent Meadow Route (gray) runs east on a narrow road through the grove, also for free. The Visalia Route (blue) travels down to Highway 198, Three Rivers, and the City of Visalia; take it for a small fee. These comfortable, wheelchair-accessible shuttles are made possible by a partnership with the City of Visalia. See bulletin boards or visitor centers for updates, and enjoy the ride.

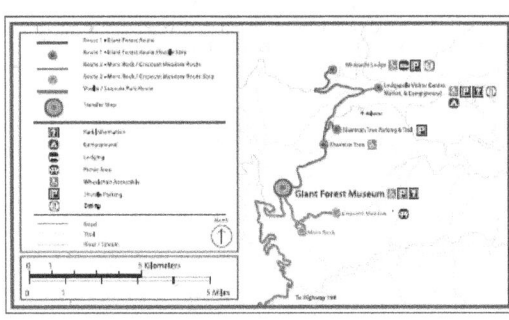

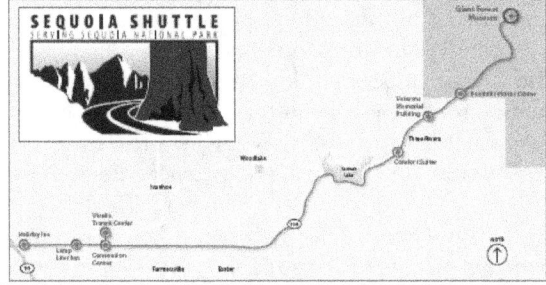

Why use the shuttle?

Improve air quality! Sequoia suffers from some of the worst air quality of any national park in the country. These shuttles use the latest emission controls, and using them lessens the number of cars on the road. Fight bad air quality and global climate change - ride the shuttle!

Protect sequoias: Shallow roots make sequoias susceptible to damage from road cuts and parking lots. That means keeping parking spaces in the grove to a minimum. The shuttle lets people park outside the grove and get a ride in.

Maximize your visit: Don't waste time looking for parking. Park once and ride the shuttle to the highlights that interest you. Get into the heart of the Giant Forest by taking a bus to a shuttle stop, then walking back to your car along a trail. Take a map to make sure you get back to the right spot.

USING SHUTTLES IN THE PARK

GIANT FOREST to WUKSACHI LODGE: Free (Route 1)

One-way ride takes ~ 1/2 hour.

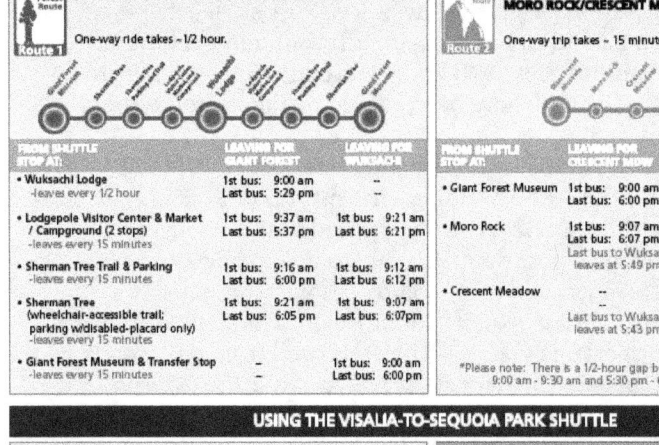

FROM SHUTTLE STOP AT:	LEAVING FOR GIANT FOREST		LEAVING FOR WUKSACHI	
• Wuksachi Lodge -leaves every 1/2 hour	1st bus: 9:00 am	Last bus: 5:29 pm	--	--
• Lodgepole Visitor Center & Market / Campground (2 stops) -leaves every 15 minutes	1st bus: 9:37 am	Last bus: 5:37 pm	1st bus: 9:21 am	Last bus: 6:21 pm
• Sherman Tree Trail & Parking -leaves every 15 minutes	1st bus: 9:16 am	Last bus: 6:00 pm	1st bus: 9:12 am	Last bus: 6:12 pm
• Sherman Tree (wheelchair-accessible trail; parking w/disabled-placard only) -leaves every 15 minutes	1st bus: 9:21 am	Last bus: 6:05 pm	1st bus: 9:07 am	Last bus: 6:07pm
• Giant Forest Museum & Transfer Stop -leaves every 15 minutes	--	--	1st bus: 9:00 am	Last bus: 6:00 pm

GIANT FOREST to MORO ROCK/CRESCENT MEADOW: Free (Route 2)

One-way trip takes ~ 15 minutes.

FROM SHUTTLE STOP AT:	LEAVING FOR CRESCENT MDW		LEAVING FOR GIANT FOREST	
• Giant Forest Museum	1st bus: 9:00 am	Last bus: 6:00 pm	--	--
• Moro Rock	1st bus: 9:07 am	Last bus: 6:07 pm Last bus to Wuksachi Lodge leaves at 5:49 pm.	--	--
• Crescent Meadow	--	--	1st bus: 9:13 am	Last bus: 6:13 pm Last bus to Wuksachi Lodge leaves at 5:43 pm.

*Please note: There is a 1/2-hour gap between buses from 9:00 am - 9:30 am and 5:30 pm - 6:00 pm.

HINTS & RULES

When using shuttles in the park:
• Keep track of time! Get back to the shuttle stop before the last bus leaves the area you are visiting. For example, the last bus leaving Wuksachi for the Sherman Tree and Giant Forest is at 5:29 pm.

• Store food properly! Where bear boxes are provided, store all food and any scented items before leaving your car. Only where no bear boxes are provided, store food and coolers completely out of sight in your vehicle.

• Park at the main Sherman Tree Trail & Parking, walk down, and ride a shuttle back if the trail seems too steep.

• Take the shuttle to a trailhead and walk back to your car rather than the other way around. Then you don't have to worry about getting to the shuttle stop before the last bus leaves. Be sure to get a trail map at a visitor center before going much beyond sight of roads.

• Take your park newspaper with you. The Guide lists the shuttle schedule, highlights, and facility hours.

• Restrooms are near each shuttle stop.

Please:
• No eating or drinking (except water) on the free park shuttles.
• No smoking on the bus or within 25 feet of shuttle stops.

When using the Visalia-to-Sequoia shuttle:
• Don't miss your bus back to Visalia! Be sure to get back to the Giant Forest Museum before your bus departs.

Questions?
• Ask at park visitor centers, check the shuttle website at www.sequoiashuttle.com, see the park website at www.nps.gov/seki, or call the City of Visalia at 1-877.BUS.HIKE.

USING THE VISALIA-TO-SEQUOIA PARK SHUTTLE

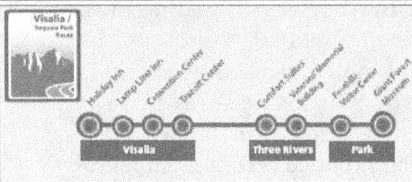

One-way ride takes approximately two hours.

TIMING & FARES

• Leaves Giant Forest Museum for Visalia at 2:30, 3:30, 4:30, 5:30, and 6:30 pm daily.

• Leaves Visalia for the Giant Forest several times each day between 7:00 am and 1:00 pm.

• Fares: $10/person aged 16 and older is collected in Visalia for the round-trip. This covers the park entrance fee.

• Reservations: Required for round trip and one-way rides. Call 1-877-BUS-HIKE (287-4453) for a reservation.

A Partnership

Attachment II

FW SEKI Shuttle
Evaluation.msg

Russ, Dean, Craig, Leslie and Monty:

Addendum: We also agreed that the Park would undertake these *additional* data collection efforts:

5. At the two primary staging areas for transfer to the intra-park shuttle system (Giant Forest Museum, and New Sherman Tree parking lot), **parking duration** data for a minimum of one weekday and one weekend day will be collected. The times when the parking lots are full will also be noted. The rationale for collecting this data is that if the system is operating well and in accordance with its design, then visitors will park their vehicles to transfer to the intra-park shuttle routes, and consequently we should detect an increase in the average duration that a visitor's car is parked at these two sites relative to the baseline (pre-shuttle system).

6. At major trailheads accessible by the intra-park shuttle system, park staff will conduct an intercept survey (minimum one weekday and one weekend day) of visitors using the trail to determine the following: (a) mode of access (i.e., POV v. shuttle); (b) If access by shuttle, location where visitor parked car; (c) If access by shuttle, identification of the boarding and alighting stops for each leg of trip (i.e., inbound to the trailhead, and outbound from the trailhead). The rationale for collecting this data is that the intra-park shuttle system provides feeder service to an extensive trail system within the Giant Forest, and that we wish to capture these mobility benefits and enhancements to the visitor's experience. Many more visitors will be able to enjoy the trail system, knowing that they can catch a bus on the return trip.

Thanks!

David

From: Spiller, David J
Sent: Monday, July 30, 2007 1:35 PM
To: Russ_Wilson@nps.gov; Dean_Butterworth@nps.gov; Craig_Axtell@nps.gov; lcaviglia@ci.visalia.ca.us; transit@ci.visalia.ca.us
Cc: Spiller, David J; Ritter, Gary T; Laube, Melissa; Kevin_Percival@nps.gov; Dianne_Croal@nps.gov
Subject: SEKI Shuttle Evaluation

Russ, Dean, Craig, Leslie and Monty:

Thanks for all of your hospitality! I think it was a helpful and productive field site visit.
Here's a summary of the *additional* data which we agreed that the Park and the City of Visalia will collect to support the SEKI Shuttle System (i.e., Gateway community to Sequoia shuttle, and intra-park circulation routes) Evaluation:

1. Construction Zone on Generals Highway – All traffic count data in each direction for each pass through the zone (during flagging operations only, i.e., day use)
2. Entrance Station – At least one day sample, counting all persons in each vehicle (and concurrent count of all vehicles (exclusive of staff vehicles) passing the entrance station) in order to estimate actual (empirical) average visitor vehicle occupancy
3. Crescent Meadow Road – At least one weekday, and one weekend day all day sample (in 15 minute increments) of traffic counts to and from Crescent Meadow

4. For each of the two intra-park routes in the SEKI Shuttle System (i.e., Route 1 and 2): Peak season week (~ week of August 6, 2007), sampling bus runs to collect the following data items: route number sampled, bus run number sampled, number who board the bus at each stop; number who alight from the bus at each stop; bus arrival time at each stop; bus departure time at each stop; number of passengers left at bus stop(can't board the bus); number of wheelchairs; weather conditions during time of data collection. The reservation system for the Visalia-Three-Rivers Sequoia shuttle route will provide the equivalent data (at least boarding and alighting by stop, including the passenger load at the time the bus passes the park's entrance station) for all bus runs (not a sample).

In 2008 and 2009, it was agreed that the sample for the intra-park routes will be extended to a second week in the 'off-peak' season (e.g., mid-June).

Monty: One data item that we will also need (see below) which we did not discuss is a table showing the inter-stop distance in miles for all three routes.

Sample Design – We plan on using a 3 x2 factorial design for the analysis (3 time periods weekday and 3 time periods weekend day), so the sample design should reflect this. The table below (total number of bus runs for **both** intra-park routes taken from the schedule) illustrates this. Data however should be collected and kept separate for each of the intra-park routes (2) and for each direction (2) – i.e., outbound from or inbound to Giant Forest Museum.

	Weekday	Weekend Day
9:00 AM – 11:00 AM	Total bus runs (5 days): 75 Sample at random 25% of these runs	Total bus runs (2 days): 30 Sample at random 25% of these runs
11:00 AM – 3:00 PM	Total bus runs (5 days): 160 Sample at random 25% of these runs	Total bus runs (2 days): 64 Sample at random 25% of these runs
3:00 PM – 6:30 PM	Total bus runs (5 days): 120 Sample at random 25% of these runs	Total bus runs (2 days): 48 Sample at random 25% of these runs

The fundamental building block with which to measure and calculate a variety of usage or patronage metrics for the SEKI Shuttle System is to construct the passenger load profile. At the most disaggregate level, the passenger load profile is measured for a single transit vehicle run, that is to say a transit trip in one direction between the two termini of the route.

Consider the schematic in Figure 2.

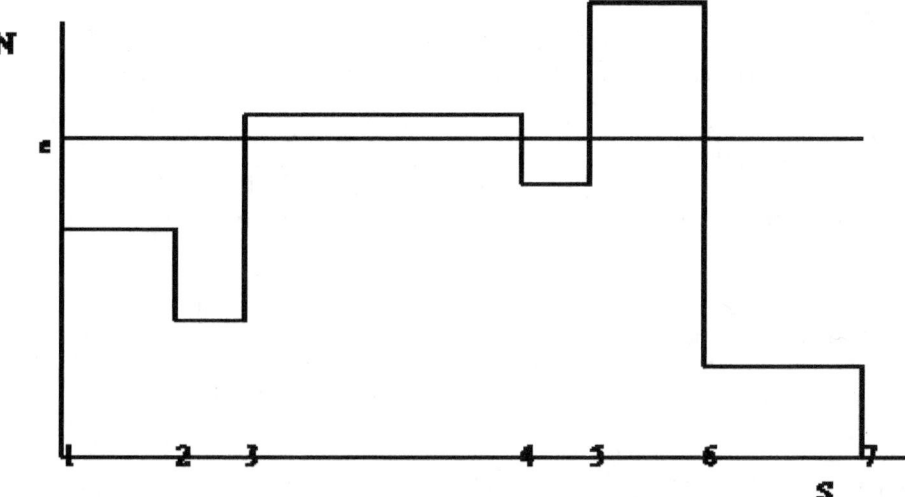

Figure 2. Schematic of Passenger Load-Profile for a Single Transit Vehicle Run

The passenger-load profile is computed from the recursive relationship:

(1) $N_J = N_{J-1} + B_J - A_J$
$N_0 = 0$

Where N_J represents the number of passengers on the vehicle after stop J, B_J represents the number of passengers who board the vehicle at stop J, and A_J represents the number of passengers who alight at stop J.

In the schematic illustrated, N represents the number of passengers on board the transit vehicle after each stop and for each inter-stop segment. The capacity of the vehicle is c. The route stops S are annotated along the x-axis.

As a basic building block, the passenger-load profile can be averaged across, for example, all bus runs in the peak hour peak direction, all runs in the day or week peak direction or combined directions, or even all runs both directions in the peak visitor season. We will average the sample data collected at SEKI using the 3 x 2 factorial design illustrated above (for each direction of the two intra-park routes – i.e, 24 passenger load profiles). A number of additional metrics and insights on the usage of the Transit System can be derived from direct inspection:

- The stop and inter-stop segment with maximum load
- The inter-stop segment where the passenger load exceeds the capacity of the vehicle
- The stop with maximum net interchange of passengers
- The stop with the largest positive net interchange of passengers (more passengers board than alight from the vehicle)
- The stop with the largest negative net interchange of passengers (more passengers alight from than board the vehicle)

From the 'raw' data used to compute the passenger-load profile, additional metrics can be derived:
- Total boarding = Total alighting = $\Sigma_J B_J = \Sigma_J A_J$
- The stop with the maximum number of passengers who board the vehicle
- The stop with the maximum number of passengers who alight from the vehicle
- The number of private vehicles removed from GTSR based on the ratio of Total boarding to the average POV occupancy

A key metric of the evaluation is to compute the **vehicle-miles traveled (VMT) removed from park roads** attributable to the SEKI Shuttle System. Because of the design of the system, this will be computed as the sum of two components. The Visalia-Three Rivers-Sequoia shuttle route operates in passenger collection/pick-up mode through Three Rivers then runs express to Giant Forest Museum where it drops off its passengers at the transit hub for transfer to the intra-park shuttle routes. Thus the passenger load on-board the bus at the time the bus passes the park's entrance station multiplied by the distance between the entrance station and Giant Forest Museum equals the total passenger-miles generated by that bus run. Dividing this number by the average vehicle occupancy gives an equivalent VMT (using private vehicles) that would have been generated by the passengers on-board that bus run to the Giant Forest Museum where most visitors would commence their touring of the park. This is why the Visalia –Sequoia shuttle route is critical to the system, since the passengers who use this service leave their cars outside the boundary of the park! Summation of the estimate of VMT generated per bus run over all bus runs yields a **season-wide estimate of the first component of VMT removed from park roads.**

The second component of **VMT removed from park roads** consists of (a) those who transfer from the Visalia-Three Rivers-Sequoia Shuttle to the intra-park routes (essentially all passengers on-board the shuttle runs since they have no other way to tour the park); and (b) all other visitors who drove into the park but choose at least at some point during their stay to use the intra-park routes rather than drive within the park to other destinations.

This second component is captured by the sample data from which the passenger load profile (averaged using the 3 x2 factorial design, and for each direction (2) of each route (2) – 24 average passenger load profiles) is calculated. The product of the number on-board the bus after stop j (N_j) and the inter-stop distance between stop j and stop j+1 ($Dist_{j-j+1}$) generates the passenger-miles for that segment of the route. The summation of this number calculated for each segment of each intra-park route gives the total passenger-miles generated by each route (for a given time period, weekday or weekend day, outbound or inbound to Giant Forest Museum). Dividing this accumulated number for the route by the average vehicle occupancy yields an equivalent VMT (using private vehicles) that these passengers would have generated. Since all of this data is sampled data, we would estimate the second component of the **seasonal aggregate VMT removed from park roads attributable to the intra-park routes** by multiplying the sample estimates (aggregating across time period, route and direction) by the number of weekdays and weekend days in the peak visitor season. Thus, it is important that we have the data for the inter-stop distances for each route in the system!!

I know this communication is very detailed, but it helps me to clarify how we're going to evaluate the system. Thanks!

David

Attachment III

Figure 1. Route 1 GFM-WUK AM Period

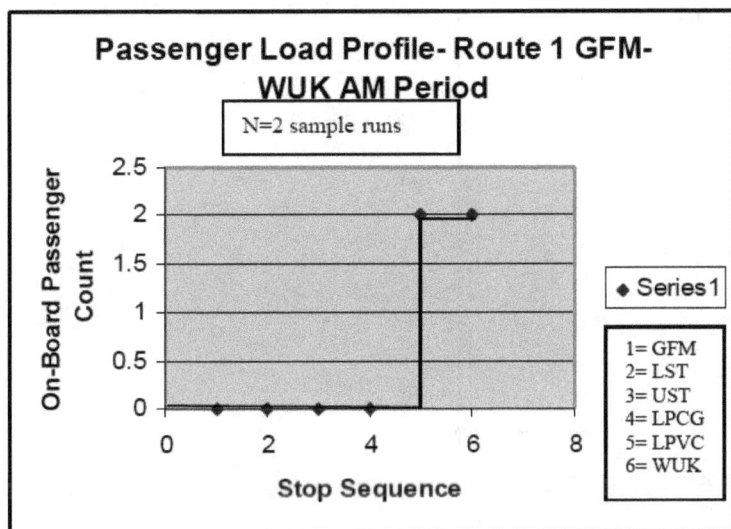

- The stop and inter-stop segment with maximum load – LPVC; LPVC-WUK
- The inter-stop segment where the passenger load exceeds the capacity of the vehicle – N/A
- The stop with maximum net interchange of passengers - LPVC
- The stop with the largest positive net interchange of passengers (more passengers board than alight from the vehicle) - LPVC
- The stop with the largest negative net interchange of passengers (more passengers alight from than board the vehicle) - WUK
- Total boarding = Total alighting = $\Sigma_J B_J = \Sigma_J A_J = 2$
- The stop with the maximum number of passengers who board the vehicle - LPVC
- The stop with the maximum number of passengers who alight from the vehicle - WUK

Figure 2. Route 1 GFM-WUK Midday Period

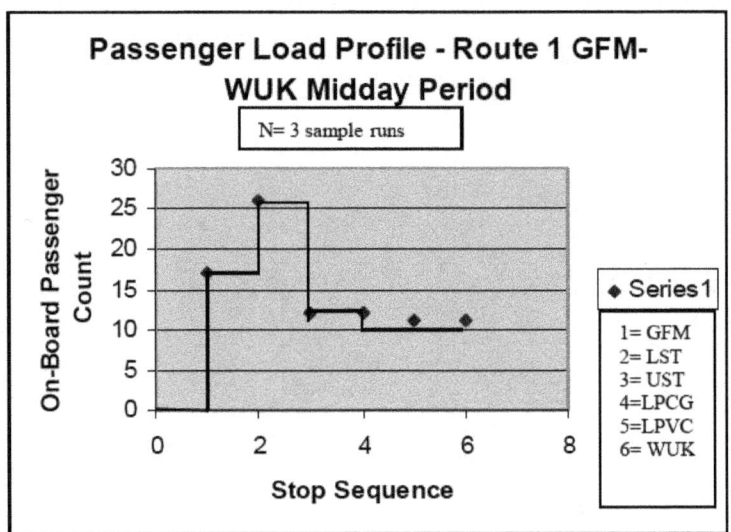

- The stop and inter-stop segment with maximum load – LST; LST-UST
- The inter-stop segment where the passenger load exceeds the capacity of the vehicle – N/A
- The stop with maximum net interchange of passengers - UST
- The stop with the largest positive net interchange of passengers (more passengers board than alight from the vehicle) - GFM
- The stop with the largest negative net interchange of passengers (more passengers alight from than board the vehicle) - UST
- Total boarding = Total alighting = $\Sigma_J B_J = \Sigma_J A_J = 38.1$
- The stop with the maximum number of passengers who board the vehicle - GFM
- The stop with the maximum number of passengers who alight from the vehicle - UST

Figure 3. Route 1 GFM-WUK PM Period

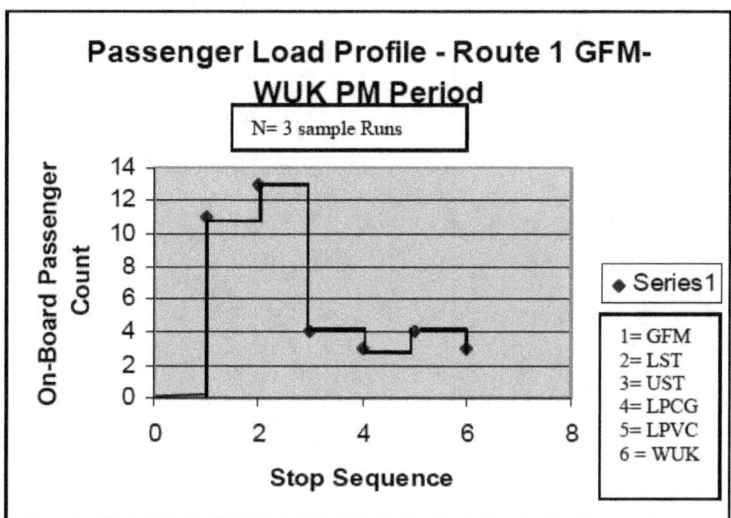

- The stop and inter-stop segment with maximum load – LST;LST-UST
- The inter-stop segment where the passenger load exceeds the capacity of the vehicle – N/A
- The stop with maximum net interchange of passengers - UST
- The stop with the largest positive net interchange of passengers (more passengers board than alight from the vehicle) - GFM
- The stop with the largest negative net interchange of passengers (more passengers alight from than board the vehicle) - UST
- Total boarding = Total alighting = $\Sigma_J B_J = \Sigma_J A_J = 23.35$
- The stop with the maximum number of passengers who board the vehicle - GFM
- The stop with the maximum number of passengers who alight from the vehicle - UST

Figure 4. Route 1 WUK-GFM AM Period

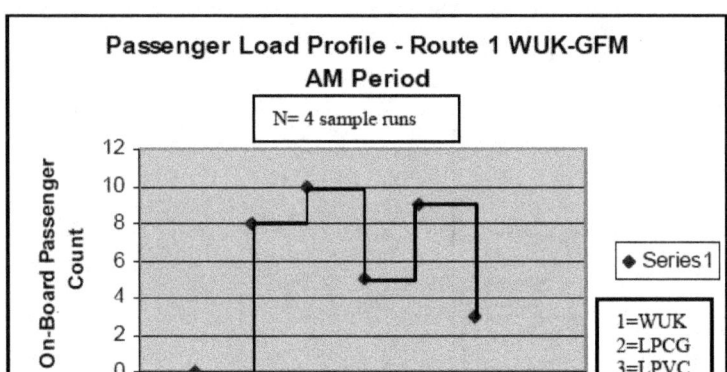

- The stop and inter-stop segment with maximum load – LPVC; LPVC-UST
- The inter-stop segment where the passenger load exceeds the capacity of the vehicle – N/A
- The stop with maximum net interchange of passengers - LPCG
- The stop with the largest positive net interchange of passengers (more passengers board than alight from the vehicle) - LPCG
- The stop with the largest negative net interchange of passengers (more passengers alight from than board the vehicle) - GFM
- Total boarding = Total alighting = $\Sigma_J B_J = \Sigma_J A_J = 22$
- The stop with the maximum number of passengers who board the vehicle - LPCG
- The stop with the maximum number of passengers who alight from the vehicle - GFM

Figure 5. Route 1 WUK-GFM Midday Period

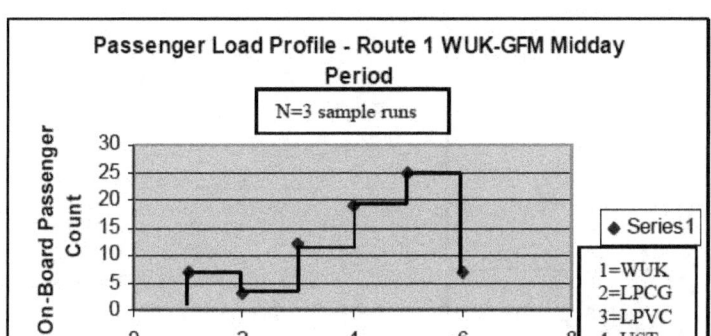

- The stop and inter-stop segment with maximum load – LST; LST-GFM
- The inter-stop segment where the passenger load exceeds the capacity of the vehicle – N/A
- The stop with maximum net interchange of passengers - GFM
- The stop with the largest positive net interchange of passengers (more passengers board than alight from the vehicle) - WUK
- The stop with the largest negative net interchange of passengers (more passengers alight from than board the vehicle) - GFM
- Total boarding = Total alighting = $\Sigma_J B_J = \Sigma_J A_J = 25.33$
- The stop with the maximum number of passengers who board the vehicle - UST
- The stop with the maximum number of passengers who alight from the vehicle - GFM

Figure 6. Route 1 WUK-GFM PM Period

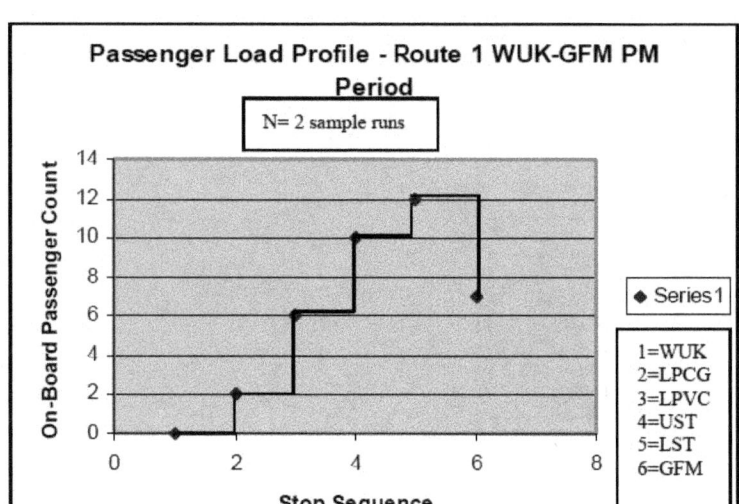

- The stop and inter-stop segment with maximum load – LST; LST-GFM
- The inter-stop segment where the passenger load exceeds the capacity of the vehicle – N/A
- The stop with maximum net interchange of passengers - GFM
- The stop with the largest positive net interchange of passengers (more passengers board than alight from the vehicle) - LPVC
- The stop with the largest negative net interchange of passengers (more passengers alight from than board the vehicle) - GFM
- Total boarding = Total alighting = $\Sigma_J B_J = \Sigma_J A_J = 12$
- The stop with the maximum number of passengers who board the vehicle - LPVC
- The stop with the maximum number of passengers who alight from the vehicle - GFM

Figure 7. Route 2 GFM-CM-GFM AM Period

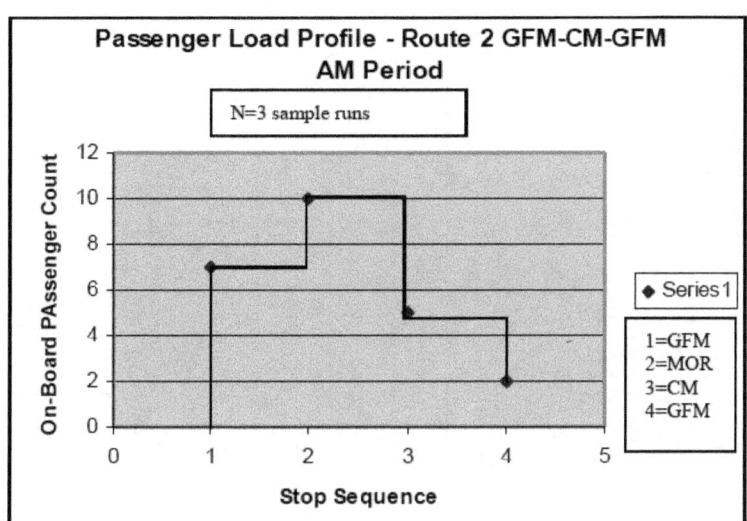

- The stop and inter-stop segment with maximum load – MOR; MOR-CM
- The inter-stop segment where the passenger load exceeds the capacity of the vehicle – N/A
- The stop with maximum net interchange of passengers - GFM
- The stop with the largest positive net interchange of passengers (more passengers board than alight from the vehicle) - GFM
- The stop with the largest negative net interchange of passengers (more passengers alight from than board the vehicle) - CM
- Total boarding = Total alighting = $\Sigma_J B_J = \Sigma_J A_J = 19.66$
- The stop with the maximum number of passengers who board the vehicle - MOR
- The stop with the maximum number of passengers who alight from the vehicle - CM

Figure 8. Route 2 GFM-CM-GFM Midday Period

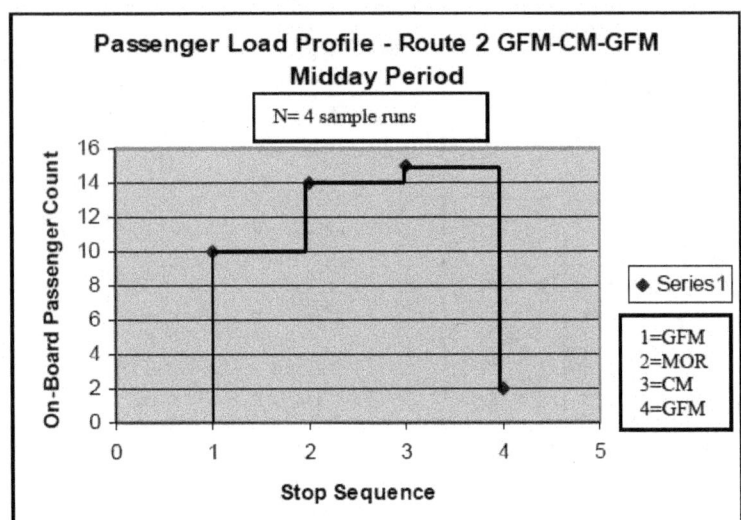

- The stop and inter-stop segment with maximum load – CM; CM-GFM
- The inter-stop segment where the passenger load exceeds the capacity of the vehicle – N/A
- The stop with maximum net interchange of passengers - GFM
- The stop with the largest positive net interchange of passengers (more passengers board than alight from the vehicle) - GFM
- The stop with the largest negative net interchange of passengers (more passengers alight from than board the vehicle) - GFM
- Total boarding = Total alighting = $\Sigma_J B_J = \Sigma_J A_J = 29.45$
- The stop with the maximum number of passengers who board the vehicle - MOR
- The stop with the maximum number of passengers who alight from the vehicle -GFM

Figure 9. Route 2 GFM-CM-GFM PM Period

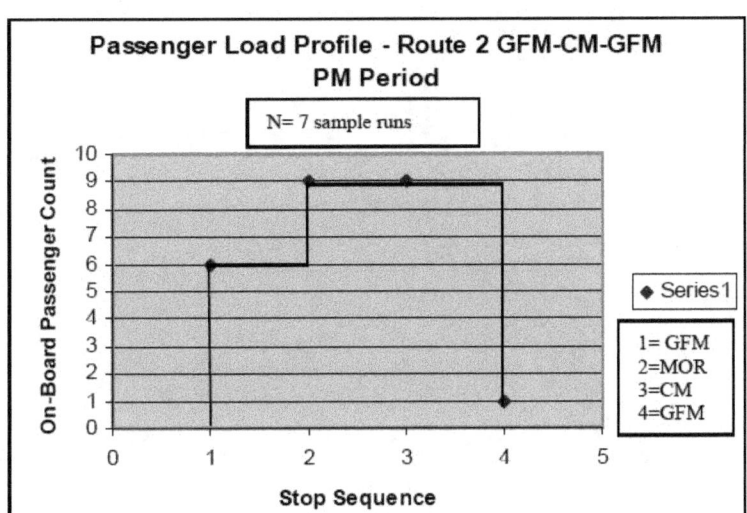

- The stop and inter-stop segment with maximum load – MOR; MOR-CM-GFM
- The inter-stop segment where the passenger load exceeds the capacity of the vehicle – N/A
- The stop with maximum net interchange of passengers - GFM
- The stop with the largest positive net interchange of passengers (more passengers board than alight from the vehicle) - GFM
- The stop with the largest negative net interchange of passengers (more passengers alight from than board the vehicle) - GFM
- Total boarding = Total alighting = $\Sigma_J B_J = \Sigma_J A_J = 14.43$
- The stop with the maximum number of passengers who board the vehicle - GFM
- The stop with the maximum number of passengers who alight from the vehicle - GFM

www.ingramcontent.com/pod-product-compliance
Lightning Source LLC
Chambersburg PA
CBHW052023280526

45793CB00005B/1107